FOOD FOR THOUGHT

Lyncia Creado

OrangeBooks Publication

Smriti Nagar, Bhilai, Chhattisgarh - 490020

Website: **www.orangebooks.in**

First Edition, 2023

I dedicate this book

*To my husband Astor & my children,
Shane, Thea & Vanya, for giving
wings to my imagination and purpose
to my
pen.*

*To my (late) parents, Nymphia and
Hyginus, whose presence I still feel,
and who guide my steps.*

*To my siblings, my nieces and
nephews, select, close relatives and
faithful friends, for shared memories
weaving a tapestry of belonging within
my poetic universe.*

*Above all, to God Almighty, whose
boundless grace and endless
inspiration lends direction to every
word in the verses of this book of
poems, 'Food For Thought'.*

ACKNOWLEDGEMENTS

I express my gratitude to all who have
encouraged me to write and publish
this second book of poems,
'Food For Thought.'

A special thank you to my daughter
Vanya for designing the front and
back cover pages and my daughter
Thea for proofreading the contents.

A mention to Daphne Gabriel, who
was happy to read my first book of
poems, *'21 Gems'*, thus inspiring me
to go on.

Finally, I would like to express
gratitude to the readers of this book.
Thank you for embarking on this
poetic voyage with me.

PREFACE

In this book of poems, *'Food For Thought'*, I have expressed my innermost thoughts, fears, dreams and joys. This collection of poems serves as a journey through the corridors of my heart and mind, providing a sanctuary where I have paused, reflected and contemplated profound questions that have come to mind.

Each poem is a reflection, capturing fragments of my experiences, struggles and triumphs, offering an opportunity for self-awareness and growth.

The poems speak of yearning and fulfilment, doubt and certainty, resilience and vulnerability, in their raw authenticity.

As you scan through the pages of this book of poems, discover the interconnectedness of shared human experiences, and remember that we are not alone in our contemplations. I welcome you to this collection of poems. May it accompany you on a voyage of self- discovery and guide you toward a deeper understanding of your own beautifully complex existence.

TABLE OF CONTENTS

COMFORT BITES

MY FAMILY ANCESTRY

–Joseph Villa

(Dedicated to everyone who once lived
there)

There's an old house standing still and
quiet
Abandoned, falling apart,
It brings back happy memories,
Yet a sadness fills my heart.

The paint and plaster cracked and dry,
The trellis work worn-out,
And echoes can be heard of them,
Who lived there, without doubt.

Two brothers and their families,
They dwelled within the walls;
Their simple carefree living style
Believed they had it all.

The wives would light the kitchen fire,
While their husband's toiled all day.
The little girls dressed their little dolls,
To pass the time away.

The sons would slide the banister rail,
Not fear their mothers scolding,
So many laughs, so many tears,
The sands of time unfolding.

This house once welcomed one and all,
Close friends and family,
Boasting of traditions strong,
For generations to carry.

The warmth and hospitality shown
To all who visited,
Was something rare and treasurable
Food, drink unlimited.

Summers, winters, hellos, goodbyes,
Happy days and sad,
The walls remember every tale
The ugly, good and bad.

The dusty teakwood chest of drawers
It stands there in a corner;
And holds a tattered recipe book,
Which belonged to my grandmother.

Phone numbers scribbled on the door,
A brochure shabby and torn,
Moth eaten pages strewn with dust
Lie on the shaky floor.

A rusted bench now sits alone
In the open patio
It recalls the intimate secrets shared
Of not so long ago.

The wooden stairway with creepers wild
Has lost its firm foundation,
The tiled roof filled with moss and weeds
Has termite infestation.

And should you hear the floor board creak,
The sound relates a story,
Of unity and close family ties,
Of youth and all its glory.

The open window at the rear,
It beckons to each inmate,
To keep this wooden house upright,
Not in a rundown state.

For should the walls come crumbling down
A catastrophe it will be,
A fortress destroyed; childhood dreams
expired,
No forward legacy.

And every time I get a glimpse
Of this beautiful masterpiece,
I think of love and labour hard
My family ancestry.

THE LITTLE FRIDGE

This morning I brought home a fridge
That my mother left for me,
A small sized compact gadget,
300 litre capacity.

It now stands in my kitchen,
It may not hold too much,
But it was left with loving hands,
Those I yearn to touch.

This fridge was always stationed
In a corner of her room,
It was her secret treasure chest,
With goodies to consume.

It stocked Mum's favourite delicacies
Like jams and cheese and sweets;
And every time we visited,
She offered us these treats.

With her little fingers frail and weak
She'd open the fridge door,
And proudly display her treasures
To us which she had stored.

On a hot and humid summers' day
She'd chill breezers, wine and beer,
Then with a twinkle in her eye,
She'd merrily draw us near.

We had a choice of alcohol
And appetizers too,
She'd package some to carry home
Without much ado.

This little fridge is very dear
A symbol of love and care,
A reminder of the good times
That my mother and I would share.

Now every time I open
Its grey and silver door,
I feel as though she's offering me
Titbits just like before.

This tiny fridge might seem so small
But the love it represents,
Is something special that stands tall
A priceless investment.

A NIGHT IN THE MARA
(A true incident that took place in 1991)

You've heard of Masai Mara,
A grassland National Reserve,
A vast acacia woodland,
Hosts animals, plants and birds.

The largest jungle in Kenya
Bordering the Serengeti,
Touching the country Tanzania
It's a must for all to see.

We were posted to Nairobi
In the year 1991,
On a warm weekend in Summer,
Thought adventure would be fun.

A Safari to the Mara
Was what we had in mind,
A four- wheel drive we hired
The strong and sturdy kind.

My husband sat behind the wheel
We used a map to show the track,
Our children aged seven and five
Were seated at the back.

The journey was monotonous,
It took us several hours,
But we knew we had to reach on time
Or else we would be barred.

On arriving there, the Rangers said,
Our lodge was the other side,
So instead of going around again
Through the Mara we did drive.

They told us that the gates would close
At the dot of six,
That timing was important
Not to get into a fix.

We also had heard stories
Of Julie Ward and more,
Being trapped in the deadly Mara
And then being heard of no more.

A mile we had to reach our lodge
So drove without a stop,
And halfway through the jungle
Amazing photography we shot.

We watched a lioness hunt her catch
Herds of Wildebeest,
The one-horned rhino,
Thomson's Gazelle,
Wild buffaloes in the deep.

The elephants trumpeted loudly,
To warn a storm was near,
But we were so enamoured
Lost sense of time and fear.

Then all of a sudden, one by one,
The animals disappeared,
Thunder and forked lightning struck,
The rain clouds quickly neared.

We tried to pick up speed - but no!
The path we travelled on,
Got filled with water one foot deep,
The four-wheel axle gone.

To push the car we tried so hard,
But all of it in vain,
We cried for help, sadly no one heard;
In the Mara we remained.

At 6pm we understood
The gates were locked and shut,
We flashed the car lights off and on
But soon those too got cut.

As mobile phones were not heard of
We couldn't call a soul,
So resigned ourselves to spend the night
In the Mara wet and cold.

We tried to pluck up courage
And fed the children snacks,
Hotdogs, doughnuts were all we had
And juices that we packed.

We prayed like we had never prayed
before
So that we could survive,
The perilous night in the jungle
To be safe and stay alive.

Soon the Mara River flooded;
Our car it was afloat.
The rain was so persistent,
We were trapped in a moat.

The wild animals were thirsty,
They came where we were stuck,
But couldn't reach our vehicle
As it was deep in muck.

That night was like the darkest night
That we had ever seen,
No stars above, no moonlight,
But giant fire flies that gleamed.

We believed them to be torch lights
Thinking help was very near,
But our minds were so deluded
Filled with apprehension, dread and fear.

My husband and I talked about
Who would be the bait,
Should a savage beast approach us
Which of us would satiate.

In our children's hands we left some
Shillings,
Enough to reach our home;
Gave them phone numbers of our friends
In the event of being alone.

At 6am the sun came out,
The flood it did recede;
We spied a tourist air balloon
And called out desperately.

In the meanwhile, like a miracle
There came the Rangers' jeep,
They were shocked to hear our plight,
Towed us out with skilled technique.

They took us to the Sarena lodge
For us to freshen up,
Said they simply couldn't fathom this
But we must have been in luck.

They told us of the danger
If animals didn't attack,
The Tanzanian bandits would abduct
And none would know the facts.

They very kindly fixed the car While we
tried to revive,
Drove back home to Nairobi
Thanking God that we survived.

16th June was the day when we
Drove to Masai Mara,
A day that's etched in our memory
And will stay forever.

OF TANSA LAKE & MEMORIES

There's a place I dream of frequently
A place I'd love to go,
To bring back sweet old memories
Of not so long ago.

It's known for its simplicity
Yet the joy it brought along,
In the Tansa lake vicinity
A holiday home for all.

The sprawling Bungalow standing tall
With balconies open wide,
Overlooking the calming lake
Where tranquillity did abide.

The layered gardens with steps going
down
To the water's edge,
The sundial was a symbol of
Time fleeting fast ahead.

The concrete banisters on which we'd
slide
Gave us so much pleasure,
Boat rides on the Tansa lake,
Simple joys beyond measure.

Beds lined along the balcony
Towards the northern side,
Where none would crave their privacy,
We put our pride aside.

Dumb charades and hide and seek,
Were games we played for sure,
Up-Jenkins was a favourite,
There was song and dance galore.

And for hours the grown-ups gambled
With cards, the game of Flush,
While the younger folk would rather
Prefer a hand at Bluff.

The furniture was rustic
All made of pure teak wood,
And the easy chairs with out-spread arms,
As large as life they stood.

The dining table ran all along
The west side balcony,
It faced the lake right down below
A lovely sight to see.

The white ceramic tableware,
The stainless cutlery,
Each meal was like a feast indeed,
With every detail seen.

I can recall the bullock cart
Carrying large blocks of ice,
To cool our aerated waters
For rupees two – a decent price.

Food and drink were plentiful
Went on after dinner walks,
With battery operated torch lights
We joked and laughed and talked.

Four generations under one large roof
All one large family,
Thanks to the generosity of my dad
 A Councillor of the BMC.

This slice of heaven we called our own
When we were young and free, Remains
vivid in my mind's eye
Fond memories they'll be.

Now as I scan through photographs
Of happy times spent there,
I see so many faces
Have left and gone elsewhere.

Some to other countries
With spouses and their kids,
And some to their eternal home
Forever we will miss.

I wish to go back there just once
It's on my bucket list,
And capture the magic that there was
Moments of perfect bliss.

PEPPER

(Dedicated to my gold fish Pepper)

We bought him at a pet shop
To learn his anatomy,
For a class three test approaching
This made it easy as could be.

Learned about his fins and gills,
Food habits and the rest.
Thought we'd keep him till the test was
done,
This little goldfish guest.

But as the weeks passed swiftly by,
We got accustomed to his face.
His radiant orange and silver breast,
His charm none could replace.

We named him Pepper – who knows why!
And kept him in a tank,
Daily fed him fish food,
While he would play his pranks.

At times to get attention,
He'd play dead tumbling upside down,
He managed to outwit us,
And get everyone around.

We took him everywhere we went,
From Dubai to Mumbai,
Got custom clearance for this fish,
Just so he could fly.

And as the days passed swiftly by,
He grew larger with long fins,
He recognized our faces,
And thought we were his kin.

Although the walls we dwelled within
We're common to us both,
His world was very different,
In water and remote.

We'd pet him through his glass jar,
His belly he'd display,
He was our sole distraction
Especially on a rainy day.

Soon we had to leave Mumbai
For the Seychelles in September,
This time there wouldn't be
Other fishing adventures.

Our hearts were heavy knowing that
We had to leave him back,
But Pepper sensed this and in no time
Bravely stopped right in his tracks.

One early Sunday morning
We awoke to see,
This brilliant coloured goldfish
Lying still as still could be.

We tried resuscitating him
Our efforts were in vain,
Our little goldfish was all set
To accompany us by plane.

THE NIGHT OF MAUNDY THURSDAY

I cannot help but compare this night
To the last night Mum was here,
 For us it was a dreadful night
Filled with doubt and fear.

Like in the garden of Gethsemane
 His apostles tried to keep awake,
While His preparation time began
For the agony to partake.

In the same way on 23rd of May
The night was dark and deep,
While we her family kept awake,
Her agony began with sleep.

Just as He prepared Himself To reach
His Father's house,
My mum got strength and courage
To unite with her own spouse.

The apostles were so helpless
They could not help Him out,
But He obeyed His Father's plan
Being a true Son devout.

On Palm Sunday a week before,
His journey did commence,
And so, we call it Holy week
He suffered at our expense.

My mum envisaged her time had come
She knew a week before,
She did not tell us of the plan
Lest we wouldn't let her go.

She had a fatal fall at home
Her journey started then,
She didn't complain or say a word
But letters to us she penned.

So, the night of Maundy Thursday
And the 23rd of May,
Will always have similarities
In several little ways.

PRINCE
(Remembered with love)

Prince, a pye-dog with majestic air,
The most faithful friend without compare.

From the first day he entered the Estate,
A lasting impression he did create.

His coat a tapestry of caramel gold,
A furry embrace, to treasure and hold.

With hazel eyes, reflecting love and care,
Prince was most certainly a family heir.

Chicken flavoured biscuits and vindaloo
meat,
He'd sniff them anywhere, these doggy
treats.

And no matter where in the world we
roamed,
Prince was there to welcome us home.

A friendly dog with his bushy tail,
Wagged it when he saw us, be it night or
day.

In his younger days, he'd bravely kill
Chameleons and cats with the greatest
skill.

And when the family would cricket play,
Prince was the best fielder any day.

His bark unmistakable, loud and clear,
Kept thieves and scoundrels from coming
near.

Prince roamed the estate like a Lord,
Could recognize our voices when we
called.

A rescue pup who grew on us,
At a hundred and five strong was his
pulse.

November 17th will always be A red-letter
day for our family.

As it's the day that Prince was born,
A soul who spread joy from dusk to dawn.

THE HAPPY TRAVELLER

When travelling British Airways
From Mumbai to the UK,
I chanced to sit beside a man
Who boldly had his way.

From the moment that he entered,
It was obvious to see,
This man was bound to offer
Entertainment in Economy.

Three carry-on bags he carried,
And two with duty free,
He moved my bag in the overhead bin
To make space conveniently.

He made five mobile calls just before
The plane began to move,
Spoke on full volume to several folks
His identity to prove.

He felt just like a VIP Seated in a plane,
And wished to be treated likewise
No reason to explain.

I was reading a newspaper
He started peering in,
Then fixed his eyes on my TV screen
On his face he had a grin.

He asked the price of everything,
Though he didn't wish to buy,

While bargaining is against the rules,
He still had to have a try.

He started a conversation,
Handed me his business card,
Then told me his life story –
Understanding him was hard.

He asked what I was doing in life,
Single or divorced,
Then gravely he advised me
And his views he tried enforce.

He gave a running commentary
On airhostesses he checked out,
Then asked for my assessment
Just to clear his doubt.

Pictures of his wife and kids
He shared on his iPhone,
Ordered for alcohol and snacks
Until completely stoned.

He grumbled at the food being served
Why the alcohol service stopped,
Eating nuts, he licked his fingers
Ate the crumbs that he had dropped.

To show his belly was content
He let out a big loud burp,
This signalled that his meal was done,
He kept the air hostess alert.

He stood up restlessly twice or thrice
To open the cabin bin,
Pulling out or putting back
Some random kind of thing.

Then propping his feet up on his chair
He fiddled with his toes,
And the moment that he fell asleep
All awoke with his snores.

Just before the plane could land
He stood up once again,
To remove his bags before I could
And beat me at the game.

He wanted to be the first one to
Step out the aeroplane,
It didn't make a difference
First or economy seemed the same.

Cheers to this happy traveller
His brazen attitude,
Live entertainment on the plane
With everyone amused.

MY MEMORABLE THEATRE DAYS

It started with the Zonals
When I would act on stage,
Directed by my father
Those magical theatre days.

And sooner than I knew it,
I was given the lead role
By well-known stage directors
Padamsee and Elaine Bocarro.

Rehearsals for those several hours
From sunrise to sunset,
Painting of the props we used
With my mother's doing the sets.

And as the curtain opened
Immense elation I felt,
Hushed silence when the show began
The audience in a spell.

The spotlights focused on me
While I would act my role,
The excitement and the energy
The directors in control.

The thrill of improvisation
The freedom to create,
The power of imagination
That never would stagnate.

The chance to be a character
Other than myself,
Although just for that moment
To keep the audience in a spell.

The cast and the directors
The prompters, helpers too,
Were all a close-knit family
A friendship shared that grew.

The write-ups in newspapers,
The glamor and the glitz,
Overnight a celebrity,
To theatre I'd commit.

But all too soon I had to choose Between
marriage and the stage,
And just before playing Evita
I closed my theatre page.

Yet there was this strong yearning,
So, I started writing scripts;
Got promoted as director
With talents well equipped.

And though the years have rolled by
The memories still amaze,
Of the magic created on the stage
My memorable theatre days.

SOUL CURRY

LITTLE THINGS THAT MATTER MUCH

What you think or say or do
Will manifest come back to you;
Hence take care what you give away
As it could bounce back, come to stay.

Though it could take a while to happen
No one's spared from repercussion;
You may not always know the source
But the law holds good and takes its
course.

Your thoughts reflections of your soul
Portray your character in whole;
Happy, kind, forgiving, mild Revengeful,
envious, sour, beguiled.

A happy soul will kindness show
It forgives and reconciles more than you
know;
But envy's etched in revenge and greed
A restless soul who could mislead.

So, when you give, give from the heart
Speak well of all who cross your path;
Actions speak louder than your words
Life's a looking glass, you've heard.

Manipulation, hypocrisy, pretence and charm
Are vile qualities that alarm;
And people see that you are fake
Be aware, make no mistake.

It doesn't cost to speak kind words
So let your hair down and be heard;
Reach out to others who are in need
Move ahead and take the lead.

It's the little things that matter much
A silent prayer a gentle touch;
They're all within your treasury
Precious gems so rich and free.

MATCHMAKING SITES

Should you look through a
 matchmaking site
It's hilarious just to see,
The description of 'potentials'
That fit eligibility.

They mention education
MBA or LLB,
Engineer, MD, or a nurse,
A chef or IIT.

They boldly post their height and build
 And what they're looking for,
In a partner for the long term,
Like searching in a store.

The bride – or groom-to-be must come
From an affluent family,
Fair complexioned, slim and tall
Single – not divorcee.

Interests, likes, dislikes don't count
These just don't seem essential,
The nature of the person is
Just an incidental.

And there are special terms they use
Which you must understand,
Wheat complexion could mean dark
And homely meaning bland.

If the person potentially is A US citizen,
The perks, they hit the ceiling
And that applicant is in.

Then somewhere at the bottom A contact
they will give,
A WhatsApp number, email address For
the affirmative.

They'll ask for photographs of all Eligible
applicants,
But are reluctant to share the same Lest
there's a serious commitment.

A correspondence then will start On a
social media site,
And if they are interested Soon a match
will be in sight.

Sometimes a person's profile Might
disappear from the file, And people just
like you and me
Think they've gone that extra mile.

To find a Mister or Miss right
But our presumptions could be wrong,
 For their names will come up again
And they seem to string along.

They're possibly still searching
As things didn't quite work out,
And probably more proactive
On matchmaking sites no doubt.

THE 1ST LIE

This is how it all began,
In the garden of Eden
Peaceful and grand.

A man and a woman created by
God, Given all they needed
Two peas in a pod.

Instructed by God of all that was there,
The good and the evil
The truth being aware.

And when in the garden it all harmonized,
A lie approached Eve
Like a snake it disguised.

With its forked tongue it told her that
she'd be a fool,
If she listened to God
And kept to His rule.

That God's likeness and image had no
role to play,
God wished to be greater
So inferior they'd stay.

he lie became graver,
The Lie said if she ate,
From the forbidden fruit tree
More powerful her fate.

So, with doubt in her mind,
the lie Eve believed,
She ate from the tree
Then gave Adam his treat.

Believing the lie,
thinking it to be true,
Eve lied to Adam
Who accepted it too.

And God from the Heavens,
saw this and sighed,
That His master creation
Had believed such a lie.

So, they were thrown out of
Paradise that day,
To survive Eve and Adam
Had to work night and day.

That first lie in Eden carried a curse,
Which went down generations
And God's heart it pierced.

And even today when we listen to lies,
We tend to believe them
And spread them like flies.

The only solution is paying a deaf ear
 Not to encourage
To their lies not adhere.

For one lie then doubles and
 triples in size,
The truth gets so altered
And easily defied.

This makes us liars for listening long,
To culprits who deliberately
Malign and do wrong.

Well, the lesson we learned from
Eve and her man,
Is enough to enlighten
That lies must be banned.

Yet how many can say that their hearts are
naive?
It began with the first lie With Adam and
Eve.

A CROSS TO BEAR

He had a close-knit group of friends
Just like you and me,
Who stood by Him through thick and thin
And all the world could see.

Yet the test of friendship was yet to come,
Although He knew so well,
That despite them trying to be staunch and
true,
They'd fail while He went through hell.

They found it hard to stay awake
The night He was betrayed,
His closest friend denied Him thrice, He
knew that was his fate.

The others too deserted Him,
They feared for their own lives,
And one for greed of silver
To the high priests led Him alive.

There were crowds who showed
ingratitude,
Wanted Him crucified,
While others were indifferent,
And coldly stepped aside.

The envious in high positions
Craved for Him to die,
But chose to wash their hands off
And instead let others try.

They mocked and spat and tortured
Him Stripped Him of all His clothes,
Gave Him a cross to carry Whipped
Him with no remorse.

He fell three times while on His way
To the Mount of Calvary,
And only one man from a foreign land
The heavy cross helped carry.

Then after hours of agony
They nailed Him to the cross,
Watched Him give up His soul to
God Casting dice they were engrossed.

And unto date we come across
The innocent who are slayed,
 For no apparent reason
Are poked fun at, maligned, etrayed.

When all is going well with them
Their friends will gather round,
But no sooner than there's trouble
There is no one to be found.

A heavy cross they carry
Their burden none will bear,
A stranger's help is possible
But doubtful and very rare.

And there are many people
Who think the cross is meant,
For every other person –
With their lives they are content.

Little do they realize,
They too have crosses to bear,
Crosses that are heavier,
But they are unaware.

If only each could humble be,
And think of how He died,
To save each one of us from sin,
The evil that He defied.

To stand beside our friends in need,
And lend a helping hand;
Ban malicious gossip,
 Be kind and understand.

Our crosses would be lighter
Our burdens would weigh less,
We'd be a whole lot happier,
Fearless and free of stress.

WANTS TO BE NEEDED

(Dedicated to my mother and every
other mother)

In every woman there's a mother inside,
A mother who wants to be needed,
And no matter how old or grey
she might grow,
She has this urge to be needed.

This want to be needed is not something
sudden,
It has nurtured and grown with time,
Right from the moment she wedded her
man,
She was needed to spend a lifetime.

Soon she's endowed with a baby in arms,
And is needed more than she knows,
From diapers to change and meals to be
fed,
She's busy and kept on her toes.

From baby to toddler, teenager, adult,
She's needed at every stage,
This gives her fulfilment, contentment
and joy,
While she turns her life's every page.

In time she becomes a grandma,
so proud,
She is needed for values to teach,
And proudly she spends her time
with grandkids,
Her advice they treasure and seek.

Alas! A day comes when she's weary and
weak,
Her body not strong as it should be,
But her mind is alert, she can think for
herself,
She wants to feel needed, you see!

Yet her children and grandkids don't think
she can cope,
So, they tend to keep her aside,
No more is she part of their
schedules and plans,
Depressed, she wishes to die.

Her want to be needed still lingers on,
Like a flickering flame in the night,
She yearns to be part of their lives
once again,
By trying to keep up with might.

It's not a dependent personality trait,
As some might jokingly say;
It's her heart full of love and
compassion for all,
That she wants to be needed this way.

Don't for a moment keep her apart,
Never show her she's weak,
She will be strong just as long as
she knows,
That her love is all that we seek.

DON'T SETTLE FOR LESS
(To my children)

Wait for the right one, don't settle for less,
The one who deserves you must give you
the best.

Follow your passion, leave no stone
unturned,
Take roads less travelled, and don't get
unfurled.

Should someone you meet tear your dear
heart apart,
Let not that define who you are from the
start.

And although it may feel like you cannot
go on,
Buckle up courage and think you have
won.

Tough times don't last –
 but tough people do,
Treat bad days like good days,
stay away don't pursue.

The toxic will have your boundaries
 torn down,
Burned, and buried, and want you
 to drown.

So, make each decision from a feeling
of power,
Don't let their actions make your
attitude sour.

These people are masterful at creating
a crisis,
Manipulative, crafty and think they're
self-righteous.

They try and gain your attention for sure,
Show them you're strong,
secure and mature.

Be firm, don't give chances,
as that shows you're weak,
For they'll know you can't let go,
Of your past they will speak.

Then pointing a finger at what they abhor,
They'll revel in your misery, and even keep
score.

Be understanding, compassionate,
respectful and kind,
But first to your own self,
keep this in mind.

It's only then, that you'll make them
realize,
Your worth and your value,
they will recognize.

When choosing a partner choose with
your mind,
Although one might seem attractive
and kind.

Your heart shouldn't rule,
for it's hard to define,
Between good and the ugly,
there's a very fine line.

There are people who brag of riches
and wealth,
Others who say they'll get there
 stay content.

But bragging and promises are all word of
mouth,
There's a good chance you'll get
enraptured, no doubt.

It's natural to think time's not
waiting for you,
But being in a haste could be perilous too.

There are all types of people
that you'll come across,
The Godly, the ugly,
obsessed and the boss.

Don't marry for pity, just think of the cost,
Of choosing the wrong one,
precious years lost.

What you see from the outside is anyone's
guess,
Screen what the truth is,
don't settle for less.

NOT GOOD ENOUGH
(A true incident of a class 12 student)

"I couldn't reach your benchmarks,
I didn't get the grades,
I took Science and Math to please you,
Though in Art I got straight A's.

And when I got an 89, In Bio chemistry,
You shrugged your shoulders coldly,
And asked who else beat me.

I understand you wanted,
 for me to be the best,
So, you could proudly tell your friends
 Of all my achievements.

But you didn't for a moment think,
Of the immense stress that you caused,
 I was locked up in a golden cage,
Obedient to your laws.

There were times I needed just to talk,
But I was shunned away,
"Back to your books, it's 11pm,
Time is slipping away."

I may have been your golden egg,
But you didn't care to know,
That this golden egg needs warmth
and love,
And understanding to grow."

This suicide note was left behind
By a student of class 12;
An all-rounder, handsome,
gifted boy Who went into a shell.

One sunny Sunday afternoon,
While his parents were asleep,
He hung himself from the ceiling fan,
Quietly, without a peep.

This one, of many incidents,
Tells of pressure parents thrust,
Upon their children whom they claim
To love, and their hopes entrust.

But the reality is, that within their child,
They want their dreams fulfilled;
An engineer, an LLB, a doctor
Or self-worth nil.

And should the child not meet up,
With criterion that they want;
He's pressurized and pushed ahead,
A first class doesn't count.

The child then loses the will to live Feels
unwanted, no-good and sore,
He gets depressed and takes his life,
As he cannot meet their score.

And the suicide note, it ended
With these words one can't forget,
Of a youth whose heart was filled with
Remorse and deep regret.

"Mum and Dad, I'm sorry,
But the journey was so tough;
I couldn't meet your standards,
I was not good enough."

WHY DO PEOPLE LIE

A web of deception spins its thread,
 For endless reasons people choose to
tread:
Truth and falsehood they intertwine
Behind a curtain of disguise they hide and
lie.

Some lie to shield from psychological pain,
They create a fortress they need to
sustain:
Others lie for gain or greed,
Spin tales of illusion for their own selfish
needs.

There are desperados too, who long to
belong,
They need to be accepted with nothing
going wrong;
To impress and fit in, a false image they
give,
Pretense is the key to the life that they
live.

While in a relationship, lies poison the
core,
They fan flames of doubt burning what
was pure:
A complex network of deceit they weave
To a breakup it leads,
Consequences not perceived.

If business transactions are filled with lies,
Foundations get weak and the business
won't thrive.
So beware of the spiral of falsehood's
decent,
Where a circle of lies will soon circumvent.

Uncertainty, insecurity, greed or pride,
Whatever the reason, keep lies aside. For
a lie will multiply, you get caught in a
maze,
The truth may be painful but forms
 a strong base.

A BUS RIDE

A bus ride is what life's about,
 It could be short or long;
There may be bumps along the way,
Or smooth just like a song.

At every stop a stranger enters,
 While one might get away,
A smile exchanged as eye meets eye,
 And others look away.

Each passenger has a destination,
Gets out when it is time;
The conductor like a guardian angel,
Directs people in the line.

Some might make their presence felt,
With strong words or kind actions;
Another will an impact make,
With a quiet interaction.

Yet few remain indifferent,
To commotion in the bus,
Don't get involved in gossip,
Won't push or make a fuss.

And while you travel on the bus,
A friend you just might make,
One with interests similar
Who's got just what it takes.

And as the bus ride goes along,
There are different sights you see;
Some familiar, others strange,
But learning is the key.

At every stop a random person Gets on or
off the bus,
And the bus continues on its route,
Through all the downs and ups.

A passenger who gets off the bus Will
tread the path he chooses,
Be it winding, long or rough terrain, He
either wins or loses.

And when his final stop arrives,
He must get down and leave,
His imprint left on those he met Ineffable
to conceive.

RUSTICATED

(a true story on a mother's lament on what
took place at Delhi India, in early March
2023)

My mind is in a tizzy
I have no words to say,
The light in our little household
Has been switched off and put away.

The darkness creeps around me,
As I stare through empty space;
My nerves are shattered,
I can't move,
Nor people can I face.

It happened only last week,
With few exams at hand
My only child a strapping lad,
A bright future he had planned.

He always reached out to his peers,
Who had weird growing up issues,
Was popular and promising,
With sound and steadfast values.

And on that fatal Friday,
I thought he'd be so pleased,
With exams coming to an end,
 A trip to Shimla we perceived.

Instead he quietly returned home,
With his head bowed down in shame,
I asked him what the matter was,
He dismally explained.

"I'm sorry I have let you down,
And caused you so much pain;
Don't know what came over me,
 But I'm the one to blame."

"I have been rusticated, Mum,
For copying from my cell,
Was only physical education,
 Not so grave to be expelled."

"These marks would not be counted
In my examination score,
But the supervisor was merciless
And threw me out the door."

"Oh, my goodness! What have you done?
You've disgraced our family, Forget the
NEET and US now, A terrible tragedy!"

"We cannot face society,
For our one and only son,
Has been thrown out from a well-known
school
For copying, he was shunned."

"Just wait till Papa gets home,
 We'll have to take a stance,
On how we need to deal with you,
In such a circumstance!"

That night was like the darkest night,
Filled with dismay and gloom,
We couldn't leave him on his own,
So, I stayed in his bedroom.

The silence in the air was real,
While he saw right through my tears,
Then sitting up, he began to speak,
His voice was low but clear.

"You surely don't know how I feel,
It's time I end my life,
For you it's 'What will people say!'
I've caused you so much strife."

And in a rage of depression,
He ran outside the door,
Reached the open balcony,
With me begging not to go.

I followed him and held him back, I
screamed and cried for help; "Please,
I beg, don't take your life, I love you,
Son!" I yelped.

He fearlessly pushed me away,
With strength that he had mustered,
He looked at me for one last time,
 Not a word he uttered.

Down 13 floors he took the dive,
While I lost consciousness;
And when they found him, there he lay,
In a pit so bottomless.

I still recall my screams and cries,
 My begging him to stay;
But filled with shame and anguish,
He took his life away.

CHILD TRAFFICKING

When in Chicago, I chanced to watch,
 An impactful film that meant so much;
'Sound of Freedom' was the name,
Of innocent lives and evil games.

Of a man who stood out with virtues
strong,
Compassion, integrity, and truth his song;
He dared to reach the unreachable sites In
the Columbian jungle to rescue a child.

There were children meant to laugh, to
dream,
But their lives reduced to a horrifying
scene;
Traded like commodities,
mere objects to possess,
Their worth diminished;
their worthlessness professed.

A hero, Tim was, for fighting to reveal,
The dreadful crimes, vile people conceal;
To infiltrate networks, reveal each cruel
deed,
A former US agent with a family to feed.

He worked undercover with justice his
guide,
Saved the voiceless, casting their fears
aside;
Through countless operations and
relentless fights,
Tim Ballard saved children held
captive by paedophiles.

Torn from loving arms, children's futures
erased,
Their innocence stolen and their spirits
razed;
Yet from hidden chambers where
nightmares reside,
Tim offered freedom,
wiped the tears they cried.

Child trafficking, an evil that stains our
world,
Shatters children's dreams and
 they are unheard;
An atrocity embedded deep in the dark,
By heinous people – those wicked sharks!

If only we could boldly take
A step forward for the children's sake;
Restore innocent lives and give them hope
Help them live, and grow and cope.

Destroy the networks, break chains that
bind,
Renew stolen childhoods, leave no child
behind;
For every child has a future in hand,
We must encourage,
help them understand.

POWER GREENS

I AM

I am who I am, Nothing more or less,
A mix of imperfections,
But consider myself blessed.

A sum of my experiences,
Of the good and of the bad;
I am my own person,
Only few can understand.

I'm not defined by labels,
That others give to me;
Not limited by boundaries,
I do just what I please.

I am a mother and a wife,
A daughter and a sister;
A shoulder for my loved ones,
A kind and patient listener.

I am a dreamer who has goals,
Those that must be reached;
I am still evolving,
Try to practise what I preach.

I am growing and I am learning,
A universe in me,
The voice that speaks my truth aloud,
 Free spirited I will be.

HAPPINESS

The very last words my mum said to me
Was, "I want for you to be happy,"
And as she lay in her hospital bed,
 I wondered
if I was unhappy!

So, I told her she needed to get well
and strong,
If she really wished that I'm happy,
She smiled and she said
 "Depend on yourself,
Never count or bank on somebody".

I gave this grave thought,
soon after she left,
And I realized how lucky I've been;
But then why was I often depressed
and morose,
Instead of being jovial and keen?

I pondered on what true happiness is,
It's a blessing that heals the soul,
Happiness is a mere state of mind
Doesn't matter if you're young or you're
old.

It's similar to that of falling in love,
You choose to dive in or not,
The root of being happy is true gratitude
For all that you've lost or you've got.

We see a beggar on the street, half nude,
Barefoot with sores on his feet
Yet he will be whistling a happy tune
Contented though no food to eat.

There are patients in hospitals with
dreaded disease,
Yet with smiles amidst pain on their faces,
There are old folks in homes abandoned
by kids,
Thankful for caretakers' embraces.

We see people without a hand or a leg
 Yet they're happy to enter a match,
A downtrodden student who cheerfully
sits,
'Neath a street lamp, solving problems in
math.

If we start counting our blessings instead,
Of thinking of those which we lack,
Unknowingly blissful our hearts
they will be,
We'll have mastered the art, it's a knack!

Yes, happiness is a skill to derive,
A therapy that's great for your health; It
doesn't require tools or another,
It's wealth you acquire yourself.

TRUST

A little boy thought his dad was the
greatest,
A man who could fix anything;
Be it his bat, or the tear in his hat,
Or his banjo with one broken string.

One sunny afternoon in the hot month of
May,
The boy ventured into the bushes;
He spotted a butterfly,
caught hold of its wings,
But with pressure the creature soon
perished.

So, he went to his dad with the
trust that he had,
And asked him to bring it to life,
The dad averse to disappointing his child,
Quietly replaced it with one of its kind.

The boy unaware of what his father had
done,
Trusted his hero much more;
He spoke of the brilliance of his greatest
dad,
His trust increased by the score.

This story sounds trivial as it's of a child,
But we too, have issues to face;
We often confide in one whom we trust,
Get sooner or later betrayed.

Trust is blind faith we have in another,
 It starts and it ends with truth,
It takes years to build and seconds to
break
Should deceit be found when you sleuth.

Loyalty and respect, the elements of trust
Are what keep a friendship secure,
Mistrust will breed suspicion and doubt
It divides and hurts to the core.

Trust the basis of assurance and love
Forms a bond that two lovers behold,
It strengthens their promise of love
 and of hope
When bliss and miracles unfold.

Not trusting your partner, you stand
defeated,
For trust brings the best out in you,
So, trust with your heart teach your partner
the art,
Of placing full trust in you.

MIRACLES

The doctors had given up all hope,
Although she was so young;
A mother of a month-old child,
They knew not what was wrong.

Prayers were said in every home,
And places of worship too;
For a miracle to happen,
 Guide the doctors what to do.

And in a period of 3 weeks,
They suddenly got a clue;
A surgery took place at once,
Miraculously she came through.

So, I believe in miracles,
As the girl in hospital;
Was none other than yours truly,
Healed when she was ill.

There are times when we are burdened,
With illness or with pain,
And nothing seems to be going right,
We think our life's in vain.

But if we change our attitude,
 Believe that things will work;
No sooner than you know it,
A miracle occurs.

The key to every miracle,
Is believing they take place;
Just waking to a bright new day,
Is a miracle of grace.

Believe you have the power
To overcome all pain,
 Believe you are the answer,
To what the Lord has made.

The change is deep embedded
In every one of us,
We make the miracles happen,
Our instincts we must trust.

If a caterpillar can change into
 A lovely butterfly;
A blind man plays the piano
Stunning all the passersby.

A tuneless violin left aside,
 Its strings are fixed by one,
Who plays a tune divine and rare,
A miracle is done.

We take our lives for granted,
Have never stopped to think,
Of how we breathe, or walk,
or talk,
Or eat, or drink, or blink.

They're all a sum of miracles
 We witness every day,
So let miracles flow freely,
They're sure to come your way.

YOU INC

(To my children)

If you must stand out in a crowd,
 Market your trademark YOU,
 You are the CEO of your firm,
So, use tact to get it through.

Think what makes you different,
 From competitors and your peers,
Your goals, your instincts, passions, strengths –
But keep away your fears.

Find out how others see you,
Trustworthy, diligent, wise,
Creative or far thinking,
They see it in your eyes.

Defining your goal is vital,
Craft a message that will reach,
The target audience on your list,
From priority to least.

Find something nobody else is doing,
What others dare not dream of,
Pitch your idea with strategy
 Don't make it just a one-off.

Be attentive to the details
Of your brand's unique design
Your body language, dressing style,

Communication skills refine.

Your target audience must subscribe
To your social network pages,
Keep updates always relevant,
And engaging to all ages.

Build a striking website
Highlight knowledge, brand and skill,
And always stand for who you are Your
value and your will.

Being published is an ideal way
To promote your unique brand,
So, write a book, create a blog,
Do everything you can.

Promote your label in person too,
 At a conference you speak;
Word of mouth – a marketing tool,
Could help you reach your peak.

Keep in mind you're selling YOU,
An absolute superhero,
A universal product of today,
That all would want to shadow.

YOU Inc. is your brand,
It's exclusive well defined;
It tells the world just who you are,
Distinctive, one of a kind!

NATURE'S CHORUS

I hear the sounds of nature's chorus
While on my balcony,
The sound of waves against the shore
Challenging gravity.

The pleasant chirping of the birds
Tuneless cawing of the crow,
And every now and then a bark,
From the dogs who live next door.

The sonic boom of a jet plane,
The loud exhaust of bikes;
The impatient honking of a car,
When a rickshaw passes by.

The swishing of the palm trees,
Pitter-patter of the rain,
The gurgle of a baby,
The whistle of a train.

And coming from a distance,
The sound of church bells ring,
The howling wind a-blowing,
 Flower fragrance it doth bring.

At night, deep in the darkness,
The old toad croaks away,
Looking out for insects,
Who hum but keep at bay.

Soon out of the dense darkness,
The sun gives out its glow,
The cock ruffles it's feathers,
And then begins to crow.

The milkman rings his cycle bell,
 The baker knocks the door;
All at once the world's awake,
 And conversations flow.

Far in the thick wild jungle,
The lion king we hear,
His roar a warning to its mate,
That danger could be near.

The trumpet of the elephant,
 The hyenas giddy laugh,
The babbling of a brook nearby,
The hum of a giraffe.

And high up on the mountains,
The skylark sings a song;
Amidst the thumping footsteps,
Of young folks who trek along.

The sounds of Nature's chorus,
An orchestra grand indeed;
Yet without these sounds
how dull and lonely,
Our planet Earth would be.

ONLINE SHOPPING

I love online shopping,
It gives me such a thrill,
To click a button on my phone,
 And do it at my will.

Amazon, Myntra, Flipkart,
 E-bay or Etsy,
A credit card I use for all,
It's easy as can be.

The array of things they offer,
From different companies,
The qualities and textures,
The designs and fit varies

Clothes and shoes and jewellery,
Cosmetics, bags and more,
You get everything you dream of,
And even so much more.

There are pictures of the products sold,
Not to be ignored
With details that are offered
So much to be explored.

The price of items bought online
 Are cheaper than the store,
With every brand available
From top-shelf and below.

The delivery date and time is set
 For the items that I buy,
And there's a return policy,
For those I'd like to try.

With online shopping I don't need
To travel store to store,
The boon with online shopping is
Receiving packages at my door!

BE A SKILFUL CODER

In a well-known company in
Jackson Heights,
Works a skilled coder with a wit so bright;
His fingers dance upon the keys,
Creating applications with perfect ease.

And with every line he sneaks a joke
A witty comment, a clever poke;
He'll write a code that never ends,
 Until "Ctrl" is sent.

But he won't quit, types line upon lines,
Brilliant algorithms his code outshines;
And often should a bug appear,
He handles it without a fear.

Searching hard through lines of code,
For that bug he'll leave a note:
"Dear bug, please leave,
 I'm trying to code,
This program just isn't you're abode"

With a determination burning bright,
At last, a breakthrough comes to light:
A missing comma was the mistake,
Seems minor, but can a program break.

So he goes about his busy life,
Making programs,
screening bugs that hide;
And in his quest, he often finds,
Life's lessons mirrored in the lines.

'For every bug we seek to mend,
Teaches us patience, makes us transcend;
And in the face of adversity and strife,
 We learn the essence of a purposeful life'.

Just like this coder, let us embrace
Problems that we might have to face,
And in the process, we'll get to know
The power within us, which helps
us grow.

THE DEBATE

Last night at dinner,
 a debate was underway,
Between my MBA daughter and her dad,
a CA.
Her dad spoke first,
his voice filled with fear,

"AI's taking over the world, that is clear.
Nuclear war, famine,
unemployment will rise,
Chaos and confusion will be no surprise."

My daughter with confidence,
countered her dad,
She stood up and said
"No, AI's not bad. It is a mere tool that
follows our lead,
Commands it obeys,
 those that we feed."
Sceptical dad went on to say,
"Hear the TV channels go on night
and day -

They speak of the harm that AI will bring,
A forthcoming recession,
stock markets will sink".
My daughter continued in a persistent
voice,

"It's a human invention so we have the
choice.
We hold the reins where
AI's concerned For it lacks intention and
cannot discern.

It's a vessel through which human
potential exists,
We control its movements;
of algorithms it consists."
Dad then pondered on what his daughter
had said,
And realized it's the human race,
we must dread.
AI may learn, and evolve, it's true,
But its actions depend on what we do.

LIFE IS WHAT HAPPENS

They were decorating their new home,
Ready to move in;
A newly married couple,
Anxious and love smitten.
But their future plans very soon got
cancelled,
When in a scooter accident,
he was killed.

Another was being treated for
 A grave head injury,
Got diagnosed with cancer,
was on chemotherapy.
The only earning member
Of a large joint family
Given sixty days to live Life changed
drastically.

Grand hopes and aspirations,
We sketch in our minds,
But destiny will chuckle,
With its own playful weird design.
We chase milestones and ambitions,
Believe we're architects,
In our hands try hold the future,
But life then interjects.

A chance encounter,
Twists unforeseen,
Unplanned deviations,
That our paths may carry.
For Life is what happens
When we're making other plans,
So, embrace each situation,
The unknown and unplanned.

HOT & SOUR SOUP

THE EVIL THAT MEN DO.

They lurk in the shadows,
Waiting to strike,
Their hatred and malice,
They try hard to hide.

They conspire and scheme,
To bring us down,
Spread rumours and gossip,
When we're not around.

Their actions are lethal,
Their hearts black as coal;
Their words sting like venom,
Corroding our souls.

They revel in acts,
Which are evil and mean,
As they inflict their darkness,
Think they cannot be seen.

Divide and rule,
Is the name of their game;
To separate a family
Is what they aim.

Yet, should we happen
To meet face to face,
They talk very kindly,
Showing concern and grace.

But the moment our backs
Are turned towards them,
They will stab with their forked tongues,
Slander, and condemn.

They move in high society With
pompousness and glee,
Believing that people
Their falsehoods don't see.

It's difficult to think
Of these people as real,
No conscience to guide them,
Attack without fear.

They can't bear the thought
Of our victory and gain,
Their life's only mission
Is to inflict pain.

And while we move on
With our heads held up high,
These evil people
Continue living a lie.

I often bring to mind My father's proclaim
'Forgive your enemy
But forget not the name'.

CHARMED BY A NARCISSIST

Charm, lies and mirroring, Affection,
sex galore,
You think you've found your soul mate,
And couldn't ask for more.

Every move strategic,
You're targeted in this way,
To get you into a relationship,
Which gets more serious every day.

Each moment of your life planned,
With passionate words of love,
They'll claim you are the only one,
Who's perfect, way above.

You're showered with much attention,
Messages, gifts and flowers,
You're taken on vacations,
Doing exciting things for hours.

The lengthy conversations
On the phone don't seem to end,
It's kind of mesmerizing,
Like you're going round the bend.

Pride and ego, they have much, These
selfish scheming souls,
There's good reason why
 they are with you,
All they want is full control.

And this they'll do quite smoothly,
With expertise and tact;
You'll think they're most dynamic,
In their web you get entrapped.

You then reveal all that you do,
And who had what to say;
But realise you have not been told,
Of how they've spent their day.

Their phones are locked for they don't feel
That you must know their actions,
You lead your life, let them lead theirs,
No need for your reactions.

And as the last days soon approach,
Their love seems even stronger,
Then suddenly you catch them lie,
They'll say that you are bonkers.

"This can't go on with your doubt
And all your stray suspicion,
Let's call it quits – it can't be right
All your drama and contradiction"!

You realise then that you've been charmed,
With vile manipulation,
A narcissist can never change
Their lives with complication.

CASTE DISTINCTIONS

He made no distinction
Between the Gentiles and the Jews,
Then why make comparisons,
When for our children partners we choose.

So, when children seek to marry,
 Why must we make a fuss?
And think we are superior,
Draw lines and show disgust?

Why create divisions,
That only make us blue,
About a person's background
We simply have no clue.

We don't consider values
Keep character apart,
Education doesn't matter
What's imperative is caste!

Being of the same religion,
Doesn't mean a thing,
We only want society
Their praises for us to sing.

Just because of ego
We mess up our children's lives,
By being so dogmatic
And insisting we are right.

For if we truly love them
Then why should we pretend,
Making caste a mandate
Won't help them in the end.

There are far too many aspects
That we must keep in mind,
For our children to be happy
A stable partner they must find.

A person of the same caste Could have
vices you don't know,
Or could be manipulative
Seeds of division they might sow.

And when we meet our Father Would we
want to be kept aside,
Because He makes distinctions Between
us and those He prides?

THE DEVIL VS. GOD

One rainy evening when it was all dark
And forked lightning was seen in the sky,
The devil decided to give God a call
For a game of chess to try.

God, unperturbed, took on the challenge
with pride,
They fixed the date and the time.
The devil then said in a voice loud and
shrill,
"The winnings are souls and not dimes".

A week later, as planned, they met for
the game,
The colours were obvious indeed,
The devil chose black; while
 God was all white;
The game soon commenced with ease.

God started by moving a pawn on His left,
The devil couldn't hide his contempt;
With scorn he moved a knight to the right,
It looked like he seemed quite content.

The game carried on for an hour and a
half,
Till at last the black king was trapped,
Then God calmly said,
"It's check-mate my friend!"
The devil with anger,
he snapped.

"You're cunning and cruel,

 calculating and sly,

And that's how you gather poor souls,
But with me you never will dare to come
near,

You're afraid of hot burning coals."

"But we must meet next time to play poker,

I'll beat you at it any day;

With the best cards in hand,
you'll have no chance, my man,

A showdown is yet on its way!"

But God in His glory, smiled, and He said,

"I'm ready for any game you suggest,
I sacrificed my son for lost souls to be
found,

So, you'll lose at the final test."

And ever so often, there are games being
played,

Between God and the devil disguised,
In chess we're the pawns and in poker
the jokers,

That's when we dodge God's advice.
The devil keeps fighting to buy souls to his side,

But God is composed as can be;
He knows that no matter how hard Satan tries,
In His image and likeness, we'll be.

DIFFERENT FACES

Last winter she was introduced
To a man with flair and graces,
But what she didn't know right then,
Was this man had different faces.

His conversations captivated her
He seemed intelligent,
He messaged every single day
Their meetings grew quite frequent.

His demeanour gentle,
kind and mild He treated her to dinners,
But dare she ask of his whereabouts
An argument would trigger.

He swore that he was true to her.
But when she wasn't there,
He got busy with another girl.
Showing chivalry and care.

The contact list on his mobile phone
Invariably was kept private,
Who he messaged, she didn't know
It was meant to be a secret.

He always did just what he pleased
Presumed she'd never know,
Then said she was all he thought about
A verbal affection show.

She's seen through him and understands
He's not the faithful type,
You live your life,
let me live mine A bachelor stereotype.

And so, she wants to break the chains
But afraid to just let go,
She cannot stand his crafty ways
Yet terrified to say no.

Now every time she is about to quit
There's a message or a call,
To say he misses her a lot
She gets weak and then she falls.

Yet aware this friendship cannot last
It doesn't make her happy,
Her apprehensiveness knows no bounds
She gets agitated and ratty.

And now, she's trying very hard
To get him off her back,
This man with different faces
A Joker not a Jack.

SIBLING RIVALRY

Sibling rivalry is a real thing,
It starts when kids are young,
By vying for attention,
Being the favourite of Dads and Mum's.

Each tries to be the better child,
By lending a helping hand,
With household chores or errands run,
And in school top ranks will stand.

When they play even simple games,
Like monopoly, chess or cards,
The competition is serious,
They'll play to conquer hard.

Why, even in a TT match,
Or on the tennis court,
They'll do their best to prove their skills,
Their strength gets reinforced.

They fight for attention and for toys, Fair
share of sweets and cakes,
On vacations it is the hotel beds,
A certain side each takes.

And as they grow into their teens,
They compete about their height,
Each wants to be the taller one,
So, for higher heels they'll fight.

Once they reach adulthood,
Their friends are all they need; Each
sibling goes their own way, With notions
pre-conceived.

They keep secrets from each other,
Believe they needn't tell,
Their other siblings of their lives,
In case a rat they smell.

When grown they fight for property,
They think that it's their right,
To inherent from their parents, Wealth
earned during their lives.

Should one of them earn better, With the
job they're working for,
The others will resent it,
And get envious to the core.

And so, this sibling rivalry, Grows deeper
day by day, And if there's no
reconciliation, The family fades away.

It's sad but a reality,
That siblings move away,
And break the bond of unity
That is supposed to last and stay.

DON'T

(A rebellious youth's verbal expression)

Don't tell me how I must behave,
Don't tell me what to say,
I cannot bear to hear your voice,
So please just stay away!

Don't wake me up at half past eight,
No breakfast will I eat;
Don't stare at me as though I'm mad,
Your 'dictates' I won't meet.

You had no right to check my phone,
My messages you read;
You then pretend you're innocent,
 And yell at me instead.

Don't tell me to hang up the phone,
Even if it's after 12 am,
You must know I have a life,
Be quiet and don't condemn.

You were young once upon a time,
 And had your fun I'm sure;
But if you didn't – too bad for you!
Grow up and act mature.

Maybe one day I'll learn my lesson,
For now, I just need space,
I don't believe in first impressions,
You think I'm a disgrace?

I'm out for dinner, will be late,
So do not try to call,
The music in the club is loud,
And I won't hear at all.

Why can't you be like other Mums,
Who let their children free,
About their own lives they go,
Not being their sole referee.

You need to meet a counsellor,
Who'll advice you what to do,
And give you exercises,
Your anger to subdue.

Someday I'll move into a home,
With my very own soul mate
You'll wish that you'd been kinder then,
But it will be too late.

So don't. don't just - don't say a word!
Don't tell me what to do.
I'm not a baby any more,
I'll make my own debut.

BACK STABBING

Why do people hate you,
When there's nothing that you've done?
To hurt them, or their feelings,
Nor tales on them you've spun.

They talk to you in sweet tones,
Then bite behind your back,
Mean words about your person,
A character attack.

At times when you invite them home,
For some kind of celebration,
Their conversation while returning back
 Is filled with condemnation.

"The drinks were spurious, food was bad,
The cutlery was dirty,
The speaker volume made us deaf,
With music of 1930"

"Oh! Did you see what her daughter wore–
That skimpy backless top?
It made us feel embarrassed,
 I noticed your eyes pop."

"They mentioned semi-casuals,
On the invitation down below,
But many men wore jackets,
While the women dressed so-so."

"And did you hear the latest,
They've bought a second-hand car,
Refurbished it to look brand new,
You can tell it's old from far."

"What do you think of the quiz they had,
I thought it simply childish,
They must have thought we wouldn't guess,
But were shocked when our team finished."

"At first for prizes they announced
Air tickets to New York,
Instead, we won a chocolate box,
As usual it was all talk."

"The return gift that they gave us,
Seems from a flea market,
Yet the label spells out Zara,
We simply just can't get it!"

"From the moment that we entered,
We couldn't wait to leave,
But attended only to confirm,
What we had pre-conceived."

And so, these nasty people
Have got into the grind
Of criticizing people
Who are of a different kind.

IT TAKES ALL KINDS TO MAKE THE WORLD

We stretch the truth and twist it,
Bend the rules when think fit,
Put others down, won't admit it
Push our weight around like we own it.

And we have people yearning,
To hear slander and pure gossip,
While putting on an act to show True
concern and fellowship.

"I don't believe it, cannot be,
 I will not say a word,
I wouldn't give it credibility
That's their business, so absurd".

And then we have the mystery folk Who
play the guessing game,
"Did you hear, Is it true?
Not a thing, what a shame."

Oh! there are the gleeful ones as well,
Who wait to see one fall,
Since they never liked him or her,
Feel they deserve it after all.

Next, we have the twisters,
Who are apt at spinning tales;
"I hope he survives the embarrassment;
He looks bankrupt and pale".

The fakers keep superficial friends,
Invite when invited out,
No mutual interests, nor common ground,
They pretend and live-in doubt.

The snubbing lot makes sure you know
You're not part of their clan,
And rub it in when you're around,
Talking about their party plan.

The sour grapes filled with envy,
Won't hesitate to say,
"We're smart we ate before we went,
The food looked bad and stale".

The hypocrites will profess to be
Empathetic and kind,
But once they get your story out,
Will bad mouth you behind.

It takes all kinds to make the world,
What we do is not enough,
All we need is to live and learn
To stand up and be tough.

SNAKES & LADDERS

The game of Snakes and Ladders
Tells us of our lives,
A journey filled with twists and turns,
We fall or we can thrive.

We cast the dice and with every step
For progress we will aim,
A ladder takes us to the top,
But a snake's head will defame.

The ladders stand for triumph,
Our efforts and luck align,
Sweet taste of victory in our hands,
The fruits of our design.

But snakes are waiting to strike us down,
With evil schemes and vile,
And so, we need to be alert,
Play safe don't lose our style.

We learn to be resilient,
Through setbacks that may be,
In the process we get moulded,
Into better human beings.

And when faced with uncertainty,
There's a truth that we can find,
Through our winnings and our losses
Satisfaction of a kind.

That life is not only defined,
By highs and lows and gains,
But by priceless moments that we spent,
Just knowing we played the game.

www.ingramcontent.com/pod-product-compliance
Lightning Source LLC
Chambersburg PA
CBHW041559160726
48006CB00042B/2155